Chapter 12

Science in Our World

Discovery Channel School Student DVD

online Student Edition
pearsonsuccessnet.com

You Will Discover

- what tools and machines are used to farm and build.
- that tools and machines are used to communicate.

Build Background

How does technology help people?

technology

simple machine

wheel and axle

wedge

Chapter 12 Vocabulary

technology page 343

simple machine page 356

wedge page 356

wheel and axle page 356

screw page 358

lever page 358

pulley page 358

inclined plane page 359

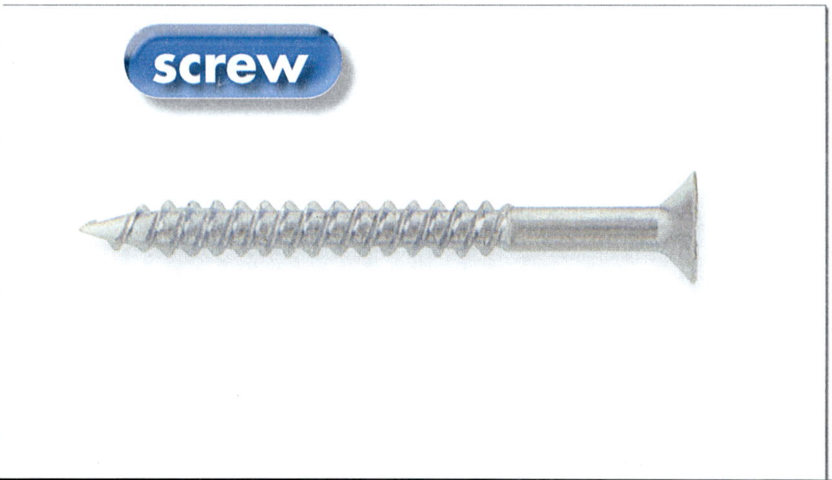

Lab zone Directed Inquiry

Explore How can you use tools?

A tool can help you do a task.

Materials

4 blocks

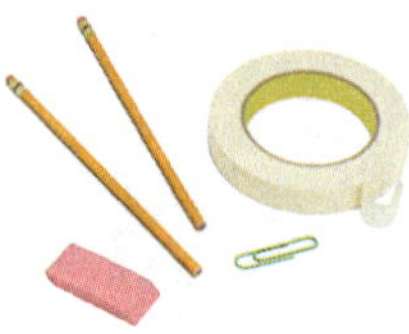

tools

What to Do

1. Use tools to stack blocks. Do not touch the blocks.
2. Try using different tools.

Process Skills

You can **communicate** by drawing pictures.

Explain Your Results

Communicate Tell how you used the tools. Draw what you did first, next, and last.

How to Read Science

Reading Skills

Put Things in Order

You tell what happens first, next, then, and last when you put things in order.

Science Diagram

Blocks

Sara built a block tower. First, she put two blue blocks on a table. Next, she put two yellow blocks on top of the blue blocks. Then, she put two green blocks on top of the yellow blocks. Last, she put an orange block on top.

Apply It!

Communicate Tell which blocks come first, next, then, and last.

First → Next → Then → Last

You Are There

Technology Helps

Sung to the tune of "On Top of Old Smokey"
Lyrics by Gerri Brioso & Richard Freitas/The Dovetail Group, Inc.

Technology helps all
The farmers I know,
To make their work easier
Than a long time ago.

Lesson 1

How do farmers use technology to grow food?

Some food comes from lakes or oceans.
Some food comes from the land.
Farmers grow some food.

Machines help farmers grow food.
Machines are one kind of technology.
Technology is the use of scientific knowledge to solve problems.

Farmers use machines to grow wheat. Wheat is used to make bread.

Planting and Growing Corn

It is time to plant corn!
The farmer uses a plow to get
the soil ready for planting.
The plow makes the work easier.
The plow makes the work take
less time.

The plow turns the soil.

The farmer uses a seed drill to plant corn seeds. The seed drill makes the work go fast. Soon all of the corn seeds are planted. Corn plants begin to grow.

A seed drill machine helps plant corn.

Lesson Checkpoint

1. How does a plow help a farmer plant corn?
2. **Writing in Science** Make a list of foods you eat that come from a farm.

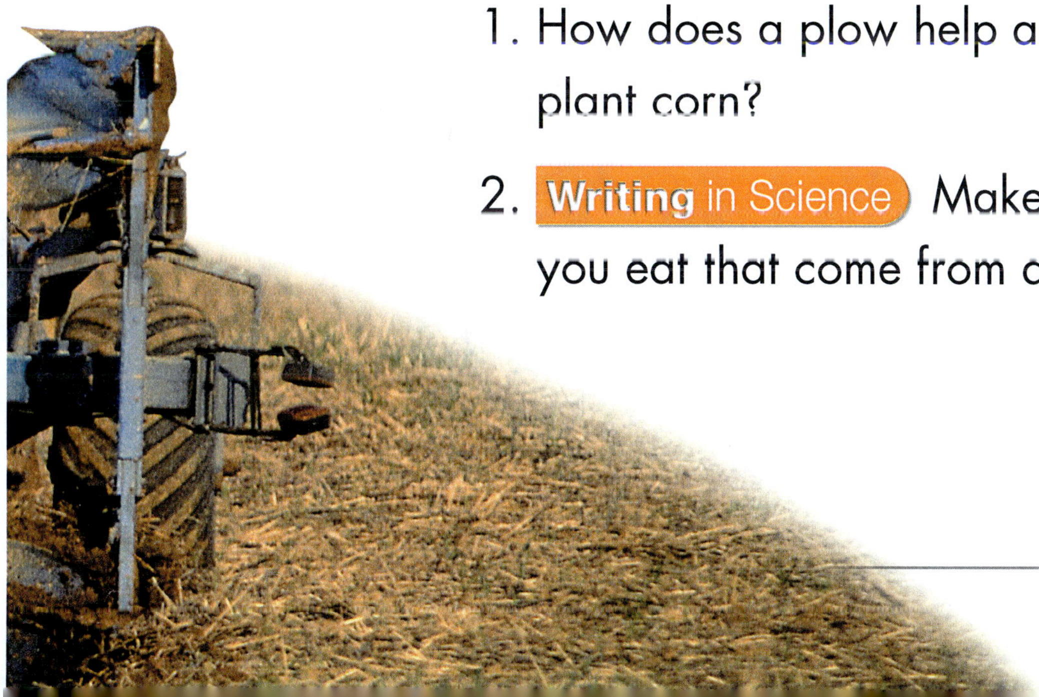

Lesson 2

How does food get from the farm to the store?

The farmer checks the corn.
The farmer will pick the corn
when it is ready.

First, the corn seeds grow into a corn plant.

Next, the farmer checks the corn.

The farmer uses a harvester machine to pick the corn. The corn is loaded into a truck. The truck takes the corn to the store.

Lesson Checkpoint

1. Name two machines used to get corn from the farm to the store.
2. **Put Things in Order** Tell how corn gets from a field to your home.

Then, the farmer uses a machine to pick the corn.

Last, you might buy the corn at the store.

Lesson 3

What tools can you use to make dinner?

People use tools to make work easier. Each tool helps do a different job. Only use a knife or scissors when an older person can help you.

What other tools might you use to make tacos and salsa for dinner?

1. ✓ Checkpoint What tools might be used to make dinner?
2. Math in Science You used 4 big spoons. You used 5 small spoons. How many spoons did you use?

Serving Dinner

It is dinner time! What tools do you need to serve the tacos and salsa?

Always have an older person help you when something is hot. A trivet keeps the hot pot from burning the table.

A ladle is a big, deep spoon. A ladle can help you get some salsa.

A spatula can help you lift hot tortillas off the pan.

✓ Lesson Checkpoint

1. What are three tools you can use to serve dinner?
2. **Technology** in Science Draw a tool you use in the kitchen. Tell how it helps you do work.

Lesson 4

How do builders get wood for a house?

Technology changes over time.

Long ago loggers used an ax to cut down trees. Now loggers use a machine called a tree shears to cut down trees.

A tree shears makes cutting trees easier.

The logs are heavy. Long ago some loggers used animals to move the logs. Now loggers use a grappler to move the logs.

1. **Checkpoint** What machine does a logger use to cut down trees today?
2. **Technology in Science** How does a grappler help loggers?

A grappler makes moving logs easier.

Moving Logs to the Sawmill

The heavy logs need to be loaded onto the truck.

The long-armed knuckle boom machine grabs the heavy logs. Then the machine loads the logs onto the truck.

First, the long-armed knuckle boom loads the logs onto the truck.

Next, the truck takes the logs to the sawmill.

When the truck is full, it takes the logs to the sawmill.

The logs are made into boards when they arrive at the sawmill.

Lesson Checkpoint

1. Tell what happens at a sawmill.
2. **Put Things in Order** Tell how a tree gets from the forest to a sawmill.

Then, another machine takes the bark off the logs.

Last, the logs are cut into boards. Now a builder can use them to build a house.

Lesson 5

What are simple machines?

A **simple machine** is a tool with few or no moving parts that makes work easier.

A wedge is a simple machine. A **wedge** is used to push things apart.

A wheel and axle is a simple machine. A **wheel and axle** is used to move things.

A shovel is a wedge. The shovel pushes the soil apart.

A wheelbarrow has a wheel and axle.

Builders use many simple machines to make work easier.

1. Checkpoint How do simple machines help people?
2. Technology in Science What are some machines that have a wheel and axle?

Using Simple Machines

A screw is a simple machine.
A **screw** is used to hold
things together.

A lever is a simple machine.
A **lever** can be used to
lift something.

A pulley is a simple machine.
A **pulley** uses a wheel
and rope to move things up
and down.

Screws hold wood boards together.

A lever helps lift the nail from the board.

Builders use a pulley to move objects.

An inclined plane helps to move things up or down.

An inclined plane is a simple machine. An **inclined plane** is high at one end and low at the other end.

Lesson Checkpoint

1. What three simple machines can help lift things or move things up?
2. Writing in Science Write in your **science journal.** Tell about two simple machines that help people.

Lesson 6

What can you use to communicate?

People use technology to communicate every day.

We use technology to take pictures, listen to the radio, and help other people.

What are some ways you use technology to communicate with other people?

Hurry!

Computers tell the firefighters where to go.

Click!

You can use a digital camera. You can use email to send the picture to a friend.

Are you at the baseball game? No, you can listen to the baseball game on a radio!

✓ Lesson Checkpoint

1. How do a camera and email help you communicate?
2. **Social Studies** in Science How can you use technology to hear news about people who live far away from you?

Lab zone Guided Inquiry

Investigate How can you build a strong bridge?

Materials

safety goggles

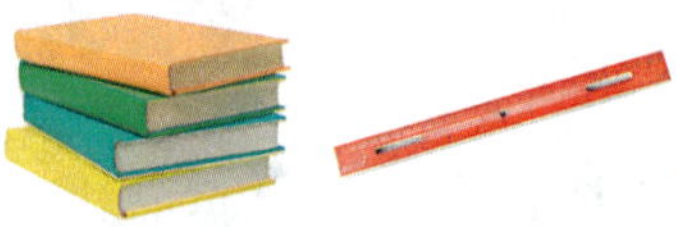

4 books and a ruler

10 stir sticks and 10 craft sticks

tape and note card

cup and pennies

What to Do

1. Place the books 25 centimeters apart.

Wear your goggles.

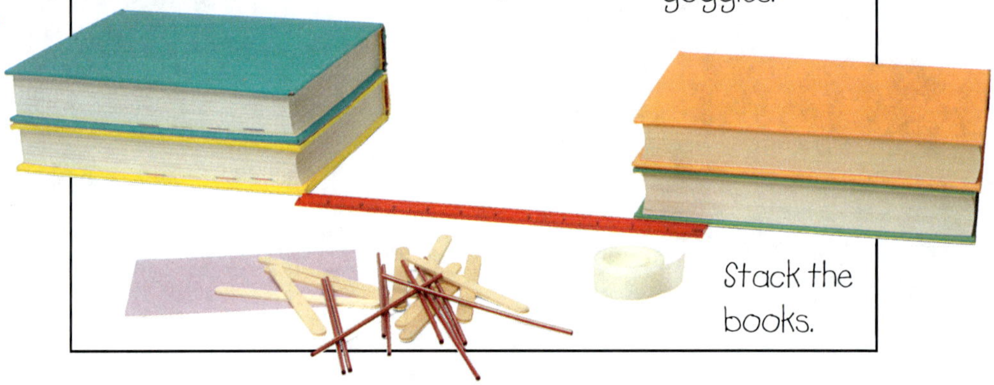

Stack the books.

2. **Make a model** of a bridge using stir sticks and a note card.

3. Place the bridge between the books. Place the cup on the bridge.

Process Skills

Making a model can help you understand why some bridges are stronger than others.

4. **Estimate** how many pennies the bridge will hold. Record.

5. Put pennies in the cup one at a time. How many pennies did the bridge hold before it fell? Record.

Which bridge is stronger?

	Number of Pennies	
	Estimate	**Count**
Stir Sticks		
Craft Sticks		

6. Try it again. Use craft sticks.

Explain Your Results

1. How are your **models** like real bridges?
2. Explain why one bridge held more pennies than the other bridge.

Go Further

What would happen if you put the books closer together? Make a model to find the answer.

Math in Science

Classifying Plant Parts

Farmers use technology to grow plants.
People eat different plant parts.
People eat the seeds of corn.
People eat the roots of carrots.
People eat the leaves of spinach.

Plant Parts People Eat

Seeds	Roots	Leaves
corn 	carrots 	spinach 
peas 	beets 	cabbage 
lima beans 	radishes 	
	turnips 	

Use the chart to answer these questions.

1. Does this chart show more kinds of plant seeds or plant roots that people eat?
2. Which part of a radish do people eat?

Lab zone Take-Home Activity

Make a chart like the one on this page. Draw one plant seed that you eat. Draw one plant root that you eat. Draw two plant leaves that you eat.

Chapter 12 Review and Test Prep

Vocabulary

Which picture goes with each word?

1. wheel and axle
2. wedge
3. inclined plane
4. screw
5. lever
6. pulley

A

B
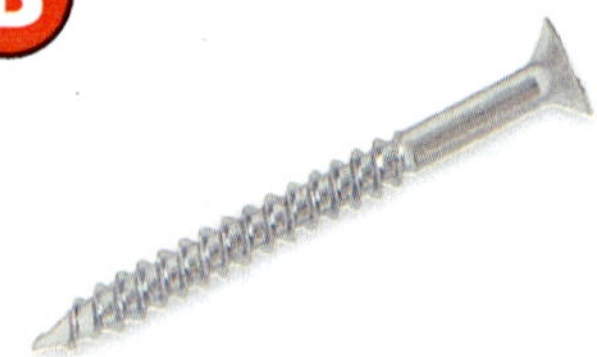

C

D

E

F

What did you learn?

7. What is technology?
8. List three tools you might use to make dinner. Tell how you could use each tool.
9. List three machines used to get wood. Tell how the machines are used.

Process Skills

10. Communicate What is a simple machine?

Put Things in Order

11. Look at the pictures. Tell which one comes first, next, then, and last.

First → Next → Then → Last

Test Prep

Fill in the circle next to the correct answer.

12. Where are logs cut into boards?

Ⓐ farm

Ⓑ kitchen

Ⓒ sawmill

Ⓓ forest

13. **Writing in Science** Write a story about two friends that use technology to communicate.

Mike Wong

Read Together

Mike Wong liked to make paper airplanes as a child. His room was full of paper airplanes. He wanted to know how airplanes flew.

Now Mike Wong works at NASA. He uses computers to find out what aircraft shapes are the best for flying. People at NASA use what they learn from Mr. Wong to make better aircraft.

Mike Wong is an aeronautical engineer.

Lab zone Take-Home Activity

Make a paper airplane. Measure how far your paper airplane can fly.

Unit D Test Talk

Test-Taking Strategies

- Find Important Words
- Choose the Right Answer
- Use Information from Text and Graphics
- Write Your Answer

Write Your Answer

Read the story.

Sunlight

Sunlight is important to living things on Earth. Sunlight gives heat and light to Earth. Sunlight helps plants grow.

Read the question.

Why is the Sun important to living things on Earth?

Which words help you to write your answer? Write your answer.

Unit D Wrap-Up

Chapter 11

What is in the sky?

- The Sun and the Moon are in the sky.
- Stars and planets are in the sky.

Chapter 12

How does technology help people?

- Technology helps farmers grow crops.
- Technology helps people build buildings.
- Technology helps people communicate.

Performance Assessment

Make a Tool That Will Help You Work

- Make a tool that can carry things.
- Tell how your tool would make work easier.

Read More About Space and Technology!

Look for books like these in your library.

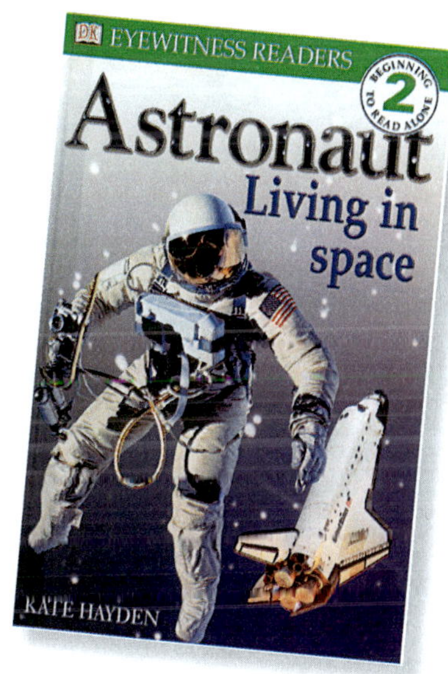

Lab zone

Full Inquiry

Experiment How can a smaller person lift a bigger person on a seesaw?

A seesaw is a kind of lever. A smaller person can lift a bigger person on a seesaw. How can this happen? Experiment to find out.

Materials

eraser

ruler with cups

toy car

pennies

Ask a question.

How can a smaller person lift a bigger person on a seesaw? Use a **model** to find out.

Make a hypothesis.

Does moving one cup closer to the middle change the number of pennies you need to lift the cup? Tell what you think.

Plan a fair test.

Make sure your cups are the same size.

Do your test.

1. Put the eraser under the ruler and cups. Put the toy in cup 1.

Process Skills

You use a **model** to find out how a seesaw moves.

More Lab zone Activities Take It to the Net pearsonsuccessnet.com

2. Add pennies to cup 2 until cup 1 lifts up. Record how many pennies you need.
3. Take the pennies out of the cup.
4. Move cup 1 closer to the middle.

Put the eraser in the middle.

5. Add pennies to cup 2 until cup 1 lifts up. Record how many pennies you need.

Collect and record data.

	______ pennies
	______ pennies

Tell your conclusion.

When did you use fewer pennies to lift cup 1? How can a smaller person lift a bigger person on a seesaw?

Go Further

What would happen if you added more pennies? Experiment to find out.

End with a Poem

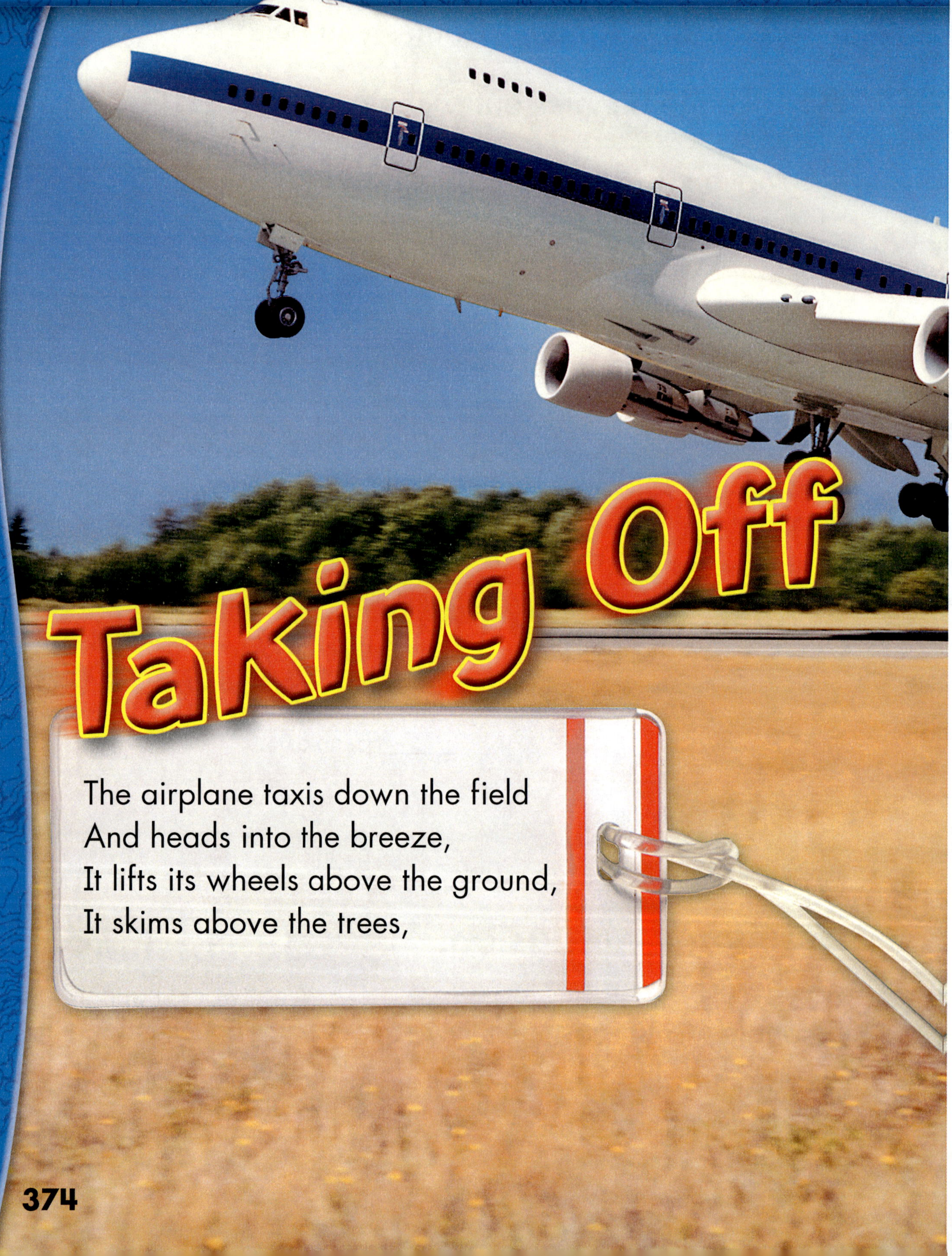

Taking Off

The airplane taxis down the field
And heads into the breeze,
It lifts its wheels above the ground,
It skims above the trees,

It rises higher and higher
Away up toward the sun,
It's just a speck against the sky
–And now it's gone!

Science Fair Projects

Full Inquiry

Using Scientific Methods

1. Ask a question.
2. Make a hypothesis.
3. Plan a fair test.
4. Do your test.
5. Record and collect data.
6. Tell your conclusion.
7. Go further.

Idea 1

Making Paper Airplanes

Plan a project.
Find out how changing the shape of a paper airplane may change how far it flies.

Idea 2

Changing a Wheel

Plan a project.
Find out how changing the size of the wagon's wheels may improve how the wagon rolls.

EC CRU 10 9 8 7 6 5 4 3 2 1